SpringerBriefs in Computer Science

T0155793

For further volumes:
http://www.springer.com/series/10028

Springer Briefs in Computer Science

Series Editors
Stan Zdonik
Peng Ning
Shashi Shekhar
Jonathan Katz
Xindong Wu
Lakhmi C. Jain
David Padua
Xuemin (Sherman) Shen
Borko Furht
V.S. Subrahmanian
Martial Hebert
Katsushi Ikeuchi
Bruno Siciliano

For further volumes:
http://www.springer.com/series/10028

Vishnu Nath • Stephen E. Levinson

Autonomous Military Robotics

Springer

Vishnu Nath
Seattle, WA, USA

Stephen E. Levinson
University of Illinois at Urbana-Champaign
Urbana, IL, USA

ISSN 2191-5768 ISSN 2191-5776 (electronic)
ISBN 978-3-319-05605-0 ISBN 978-3-319-05606-7 (eBook)
DOI 10.1007/978-3-319-05606-7
Springer Cham Heidelberg New York Dordrecht London

Library of Congress Control Number: 2014936410

Printed on acid-free paper

Springer is part of Springer Science+Business Media (www.springer.com)

*To my parents, Kamal and Jaya, to whom
I owe all my achievements*

*To my advisor, Dr. Levinson, for all his
help and advice*

*To my lab partners, Aaron and Luke,
for all their help and support*

To my alma mater

Contents

Chapter 1
Introduction

In yesteryears, battlefields were specific, strategically chosen locations and it was on these battlefields that heroes and cowards were born. With the exception of ambushes, wars of the past have a sense of locality about them. On the contrary, today's armed forces no longer have that luxury. The battle can easily start in tropical jungles, move towards an urban attack on a city and might end with an ICBM attack from space. While definitely a frightening scenario, the truth is that battle lines no longer exist and conflicts may erupt at any place and time.

In order to deal with such scenarios, the armed forces of countries all around the world are always on the highest alert, on the lookout for a missile launch or for troop movements. Furthermore, all these various possible scenarios require a lot of training for the soldiers before they can be sent to war. The training period lasts from at least a couple of months to several years, depending on a variety of factors. Additionally, an enormous financial budget is required for the training of all these soldiers, as well as for maintaining their alertness and battle readiness. However, what if technology were to play a more mainstream role in direct combat? That seems to be the general direction that armed forces all around the world seem to be heading towards.

The idea of using robots in war is not a radically new one and various militaries around the world have begun the widespread adoption of robots along front lines. Today, we have drones that are piloted remotely and are capable of taking out targets. There is also heavy on-going research to make the drones more autonomous, thus reducing the requirement on humans. There are also legged robots in development that can aid and assist soldiers in moving their equipment and luggage from place to place, and is resilient to various land texture and features.

In this book, we present a research project wherein we train a humanoid robot to pick out targets from various objects and fire NERF™ bullets at the target, using a commercially available NERF™ gun (a children's toy). The goal of the experiment is to incorporate the latest computer vision and machine learning algorithms so that the robot would be able to practice shooting at targets, and within a few training iterations, have an accuracy that can at least match or exceed trained soldiers. In the case of a miss, the robot should be able to determine the magnitude of its error and

V. Nath and S.E. Levinson, *Autonomous Military Robotics*, SpringerBriefs in Computer Science, DOI 10.1007/978-3-319-05606-7_1, © The Author(s) 2014

automatically correct itself so that the next shot would have a much greater probability of hitting the target. By training the robot over a wide variety of scenarios, it is possible to fine-tune the AI algorithms to a level where the robot has an accuracy of >90 %.

The robot that was used during the experimental setup was a humanoid robot called the iCub. It is a robot that has been developed by the European Union and is capable of cognitive development like a 3 year old human child (Sandini, Metta, & Vernon, 2007). The goal of the iCub is to advance the current understanding of natural and artificial cognitive systems. In the experiment, we used the NERF™ gun for safety purposes as well as for legal reasons. However, the work presented in this book is adaptable to a real gun. The main thing that would change would be the grasp of the robot's hand on the gun, its relative positioning and accounting for recoil. These are trivial issues and can be accounted for relatively easily.

Using more robots in war is definitely going to be more advantageous than the present day scenarios. Robots would dutifully obey every command and would never suffer from fatigue, sleep deprivation, lack of stamina, bruises and injuries and other factors that human beings are prone to. However, there is the concern that such robots could result in oppression of the people and be used to carry out non-ethical and/or illegal activities. In spite of engineering several safety mechanisms in the robots, the requirement of customization will always create a loop hole in these mechanisms. The only true way to prevent any such calamity would be to ensure a proper safety mechanism that is staffed by humans to ensure that no person can misuse the power of such devastating weapons.

References

Asimov, I. (1991). *I, Robot*. New York, NY: Spectra, Mti Edition.

Breazeal, C., Wang, A., & Picard, R. (2007). *Experiments with a robotic computer: Body, affect and cognition interactions. HRI'07* (pp. 153–160). Arlington, VA: ACM.

Buşoniu, L., Babuška, R., De Schutter, B., & Ernst, D. (2010). *Reinforcement learning and dynamic programming using function approximators*. New York, NY: CRC Press.

Forsyth, D., & Ponce, J. (2011). *Computer vision: A modern approach*. Upper Saddle River, NJ: Prentice Hall.

Harnad, S. (1995). *Grounding symbolic capacity in robotic capacity*. New Haven, CT: Lawrence Erlbaum.

Kormushev, P., Calinon, S., Saegusa, R., & Metta, G. (2010). Learning the skill of archery by a humanoid iCub. *2010 IEEE-RAS International Conference on Humanoid Robotics*. Nashville.

Metta, G., Sandini, G., Vernon, D., & Natale, L. (2008). The iCub humanoid robot: An open platform for research in embodied cognition. *8th Workshop on performance metrics for intelligent systems*. ACM.

Nath, V., & Levinson, S. (2013a). *Learning to fire at targets by an iCub Humanoid Robot. AAAI Spring Symposium*. Palo Alto, CA: AAAI.

Nath, V., & Levinson, S. (2013b). *Usage of computer vision and machine learning to solve 3D mazes*. Urbana, IL: University of Illinois at Urbana-Champaign.

Nath, V., & Levinson, S. (2014). Solving 3D Mazes with Machine Learning: A prelude to deep learning using the iCub Humanoid Robot. *Twenty-Eighth AAAI Conference*. Quebec City: AAAI

Russell, S., & Norvig, P. (2010). *Artificial intelligence, a modern approach*. Upper Saddle River, NJ: Prentice Hall.

Sandini, G., Metta, G., & Vernon, G. (2007). The iCub cognitive humanoid robot: An open-system research platform for enactive cognition. In *50 Years of artificial intelligence* (pp. 358–369). Berlin: Springer.

Spong, M. W., Hutchinson, S., & Vidyasagar, M. (2006). *Robot modelling and control*. Hoboken, NJ: John Wiley & Sons.

Sutton, R. S., & Barto, A. G. (1998). *Reinforcement learning: An introduction*. Cambridge, MA: MIT Press.

Tsagarakis, N., Metta, G., & Vernon, D. (2007). iCUb: The design and realization of an open humanoid platform for cognitive and neuroscience research. *Advanced Robots, 21*(10), 1151–1175.

Wells, H. (2005). *The war of the worlds*. New York, NY: NYRB Classics.

Chapter 2
Overview of Probability and Statistics

Abstract This chapter talks about the elementary concepts of probability and statistics that are needed to better comprehend this book. This appendix covers topics like basic probability, conditional probability, Bayes' Theorem and various distributions like normal distribution (also called Gaussian distribution), Bernoulli distribution, Poisson distribution and binomial distribution.

2.1 Probability

2.1.1 Introduction

The world that we observe is a very complex one, with an infinite number of events taking place all the time, some of which are interdependent/related and some of which are independent of certain events. These events can be divided into two categories—(1) Deterministic, (2) Probabilistic. Deterministic events are those events that we are sure will happen, given the right conditions. It is the notion of cause-and-effect, in that an event A will lead to event B, when the right conditions are applied to event A. Strictly speaking, deterministic events are usually considered more of a philosophical concept than a practical one since it is impossible to predict an event with complete accuracy and confidence. There are too many variables at play in the interaction of even two systems, let alone several hundreds or thousands of them, and it would be impossible to predict the relationship between every single one of them.

However, it is important to note that the choice of granularity would depend on the event and the level of detail that the system being analyzed warrants. For example, it would be quite pointless to include calculations of atomic vibrations while flipping a biased coin, one that has heads on both sides. In this scenario, the event that the coin will result in heads can be considered a deterministic event, since we are absolutely sure that the coin will result in a heads.

The other event category are the probabilistic events. These events describe real-life scenarios more accurately because they mention the probability that an event will occur. The probability of likely events will be higher than those of unlikely events, and this variation is the measure of probability. The measure of probability is bounded by (2.1).

$$0 \leq P(X) \leq 1 \tag{2.1}$$

The "X" in (2.1) refers to any event X. P(X) is the notation to indicate the probability of an event "X". Equation (2.1) indicates that the minimum value of probability of any event is 0, while the maximum probability of an event is 1. This means that if an event is deemed impossible, its probability is 0, while the probability of an event that has no way of failing will be a 1.

So, what is probability? Generally speaking, probability can be thought of as the likelihood of a particular event happening. Most of us have a model of probability affecting our daily lives. For instance, we tend to look at the probability that it would rain today before deciding on taking an umbrella or not. We also use probability in a lot of trading places like the stock market. Also, the period of warranty that manufacturers indicate for a new product is an indication of the probability that the device would function for a particular duration. The probability of the device failing within the warranty period is low, and that is why the manufacturer decided to cover only up to a certain period and not for an indefinite period.

Now that we have an understanding of what is probability, let us discuss how to mathematically determine the probability of a particular event. To do this, consider one of the most widely used objects to teach probability—the board games' die. When we roll a die, there are only six numbers that can be obtained, namely 1, 2, 3, 4, 5 and 6. Representing them as a set would result in the set $\{1, 2, 3, 4, 5, 6\}$. Such a set that contains all the possible results of a particular event is called a **power set**. Thus, the set $\{1, 2, 3, 4, 5, 6\}$ is the power set of the event of rolling a fair die. As an example, to determine the probability of rolling a 4 on a die can be determined as follows:

$$P(A) = \frac{\{4\}}{\{1, 2, 3, 4, 5, 6\}} = \frac{1}{6}$$

Basically, we need to have the events in the numerator and the total number of events in the denominator. As can be seen from the above equation, the probability of the die landing a 4 is 1/6. As you might have figured out by now, the probability of any number landing when a fair die is thrown is the same, i.e. 1/6. This means that when you throw a fair die, you are equally likely to get any of the 6 numbers marked on it.

As another commonly cited example, let us consider an ordinary coin. This coin will have two sides—a heads and a tails. What is the probability that the coin will yield heads when it is tossed? The power set of coin toss is {H, T}, where H denotes heads and T denotes tails. In this scenario,

$$P(A) = \frac{\{H\}}{\{H,T\}} = \frac{1}{2}$$

where A is the event that the coin toss will yield a heads. By a similar analysis, we can determine that the probability of a coin toss yielding a tails would also be 1/2. In other words, both the outcomes have an equal probability. Another crucial observation that can be made from both examples is that the sum of the probabilities of all the events must equal 1. This is a rule in probability and can be observed from the coin toss experiment mentioned above. The sum of both probabilities is $1/2 + 1/2 = 1$. The same can be observed from the die experiment. The mathematical notation of this rule is given by (2.2) below.

$$\sum_i P(x_i) = 1. \qquad (2.2)$$

In (2.2) above, i refers to the individual events, i.e. subsets of the power set. The summation of all the individual elements would result in the power set for the event.

On a related note, there is another concept called complementary events that are a direct result of (2.2). A complementary event is an event wherein its negative will take place. For example, if an event A is defined as landing a 4 on a die roll, it's complementary event, A', would be NOT landing a 4 on a die roll. Since the sum of all the probability events must be 1, from (2.2),

$$P\left(A'\right) = 1 - P(A) = 1 - 1/6 = 5/6$$

That is, there is a 5 in 6 chance that the number obtained would not be a 4. This is in agreement with simple observation since the resultant set is {1, 2, 3, 5, 6}.

2.1.2   Conditional Probability and Bayes' Theorem

Now that we know the basics of probability, let's take a look at the topic conditional probability. Basically, conditional probability is the probability of an event when another related event has taken place. This knowledge of another related event taking place will affect our probability of the first event, and this concept is called conditional probability, in that it is the probability given a particular condition.

Let us consider the example of the die once again. The power set for an ordinary die is {1, 2, 3, 4, 5, 6} and the probability of getting any number from 1 to 6 on a single throw is the same 1/6. However, what if I were to tell you that the die has been tampered with and that this die now contains only even numbers on it? With this new information, wouldn't the probabilities change? It surely does! In this new scenario, the power set of the die is $\{2, 4, 6\}$. Therefore, the probability of getting a 1, 3 or 5 is 0. The probability of getting a 2, 4, or 6 is 1/3. The notation for representing conditional probability is given by $P(A|B)$ and is read as "probability of A given B". So, if we were to formalize the example we just discussed, it would be as follows:

A : Getting a 2 on a die roll

B : The die contains only even numbers

Therefore, $P(A|B) = 1/3$. While this approach of counting the events that satisfy a particular condition and are members of the power set might work for events with a limited number of outcomes, this approach would quickly get out of hand when we have to deal with a large number of events. It is here that the formula for conditional probability comes in handy. The formula for computing the conditional probability is given below as (2.3).

$$P(A|B) = \frac{P(A \cap B)}{P(B)} \tag{2.3}$$

To demonstrate the usage of (2.3) for determining conditional probability, let us use an example of an octahedron. An octahedron differs from a regular die in only a very small way, a regular die has six sides, while an octahedron has eight sides. So, the numbers marked on an octahedron range from 1 to 8, as opposed to 1–6 on a regular die.

Now, let us define the two events A and B as follows:

A : Getting an even number on a roll

B : Getting a number greater than 6, non-inclusive

The power set of all the rolls from an octahedron is $\{1, 2, 3, 4, 5, 6, 7, 8\}$. The probability of A = 1/2, since there is an equal chance of the roll landing in an odd or even number (the reader can also confirm this by listing all the even numbers and the power set). The set of outcomes that satisfy event B is $\{7, 8\}$. This means that the probability of B is 2/8 = 1/4. The intersection of events A and B leads to the resultant set $\{8\}$. This set satisfies both events A and B. The probability of A ∩ B = 1/8. Thus, the application of (2.3) results in the following:

$$P(A|B) = \frac{P(A \cap B)}{P(B)} = \frac{1/8}{2/8} = \frac{1}{2}$$

In this example, it so happened that $P(A|B) = P(A)$. But this is not always necessarily true. Similarly, in this example, $P(B|A) = P(B)$ as well. When such a condition occurs, we say that the two events A and B are **statistically independent** of each other. This means that the probability of occurrence of one event is completely independent of the probability of occurrence of another. This should make intuitive sense because when you roll an octahedron, getting an odd/even number and a number greater than 6 should not have any relationship with each other. The above equations mathematically prove this idea. Furthermore, when two events are independent, their joint probability is the product of their individual probabilities. This is shown in (2.4) below.

$$P(A \cap B) = P(A) * P(B) \tag{2.4}$$

Conditional probability is a widely used concept in several experiments, especially because several events are related to each other in one way or the other. This concept of conditional probability and the Bayes' Theorem (which we will discuss next) is of tremendous importance to the field of artificial intelligence and is used widely in the algorithms being described in this book.

Conditional probability gives rise to another very important theorem in the field of probability, the Bayes' Theorem. The Bayes' theorem is widely used to flip the events whose probabilities are being computed, so that they can computed much more easily, and in some cases the only way they can be computed. The formula for Bayes' theorem is given by (2.5) below.

$$P(A|B) = \frac{P(B|A) * P(A)}{P(B)} \tag{2.5}$$

As can be seen from (2.5), in the original problem we tried to compute the probability of A given B. Bayes' theorem allows us to compute this by first computing the probability of B given A, along with the individual probabilities of A and B. The Bayes' theorem of (2.5) has another form, which is given by (2.6) below.

$$P(A|B) = \frac{P(B|A) * P(A)}{P(B)} = \frac{P(B|A) * P(A)}{P(B|A) * P(A) + P(B|A') * P(A')} \tag{2.6}$$

Equation (2.6) is obtained from (2.5) by the expansion of P(B) in the denominator. This takes place because the probability of an event needs to account for the conditional probabilities of the event occurring as well as the event not occurring (complementary events). The Bayes' theorem is one of the most important theorems being used in the field of artificial intelligence, since almost all of AI deals with probabilistic events, and not deterministic events.

2.2   Probability Distributions

In this section, we will be discussing the most commonly used probability distributions. The distributions that we will discuss are Gaussian distribution, binomial distribution, Bernoulli distribution and Poisson distribution. Of course, there are various other distributions, but they are not required for an understanding of the work presented in this book and have been ignored.

Before we proceed with the distributions, there are two concepts that need to be explained to the reader to better understand the material. The first concept is that of probability mass function (PMF), while the second is called the cumulative distribution function (CDF).

PMF is a function which maps a discrete random variable as input to its corresponding probability as an output. This function is used when the inputs are purely discrete in nature (Weisstein). For example, the ordinary 6-sided die that we discussed about has an input that is discrete in nature, i.e. it is guaranteed to be a natural number between 1 and 6. As shown previously, the probability of each of the inputs being obtained for a fair die is equal, which is 1/6. Thus, if one were to plot the pmf of the inputs of a die, it would be 6 equal line segments that represent a value of 1/6 each. Similarly, for a single fair coin toss, the only two outcomes would be heads and tails. Therefore, if we were to obtain the pmf of this event, it would be 2 equal line segments that represent a value of 1/2 each.

CDF is a similar function as PMF, with the difference that this function gives the sum of all the possible probabilities until that event has been reached. For continuous functions, the CDF would range from negative infinity to the point where the current event of interest has been obtained/plotted on the graph (Weisstein, "Distribution Functions"). Both the PMF and CDF have been shown in the distributions being discussed for certain cases, as an example.

2.2.1   Gaussian Distribution

The Gaussian distribution is one of the most commonly used probability distribution function, and is also called the normal distribution. The Gaussian distribution is also referred to as the bell curve because of the shape of the PMF function of the normal distribution (the bell curve has a lot of applications while grading tests since professors tend to "curve" the grades based on overall class performance). The Gaussian distribution has a number of parameters that are needed to accurately model it. The first one is μ, which is also called the *mean* of the distribution. The mean is the sum of all the random variables in the distribution times the probability of each of the random variables. This can be represented in equation form below, as (2.7).

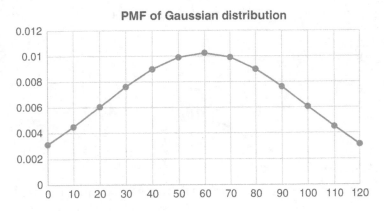

Fig. 2.1 PMF of Gaussian distribution

$$\mu = \sum_x x\,P(x) \tag{2.7}$$

The other parameter is σ, the *standard deviation* of the distribution. Standard deviation is a measure of the variation of the members of the distribution from the mean and is given by (2.8).

$$\sigma = \sqrt{\frac{1}{N}\sum_{i=1}^{N}(x_i - \mu)^2} \tag{2.8}$$

In (2.8), each value of x is a member of the distribution. σ^2 is also called the *variance* of the distribution.

Now that we have the required parameters to accurately represent the Gaussian distribution, the PMF of a Gaussian distribution is given by (2.9), while the CDF is given by (2.10) below (Weisstein, "Normal Distribution").

$$PMF = \frac{1}{\sigma\sqrt{2\pi}}e^{\frac{-(x-\mu)^2}{2\sigma^2}} \tag{2.9}$$

$$CDF = \frac{1}{2}\left[1 + \mathrm{erf}\left(\frac{x-\mu}{\sqrt{2\sigma^2}}\right)\right] \tag{2.10}$$

Figures 2.1 and 2.2 below show the PMF and CDF of a Gaussian distribution.

One last thing before concluding the section on Gaussian distribution, when μ = 0 and σ = 1, the distribution can also be called the *standard normal distribution*.

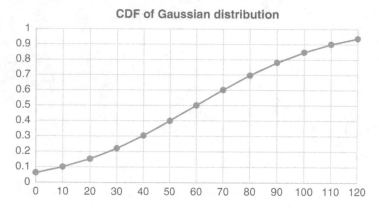

Fig. 2.2 CDF of Gaussian distribution

2.2.2 Binomial Distribution

The binomial distribution is another type of distribution that is very commonly encountered when the same experiment is repeated several times. The experiment is of the pass/fail or yes/no type, where the probability of success is denoted by a parameter, say "p". Since the outcome of these experiments is comprised of two possibilities, the probability of failure would be $1 - p$. This is because of the complementary nature of the success and failure of the events.

The binomial distribution is the distribution used to model the repeated tossing of a coin, rolling a die, or any other such experiment, where it would be extremely hard to model the event using other models. The PMF of a binomial distribution is given by (2.11) below (Weisstein, "Binomial Distribution").

$$PMF = {}^{n}_{s}C\, p^{s}(1 - p)^{n-s} \tag{2.11}$$

In (2.11), s is the number of successes that the experiment yielded, or we would like to yield. Since the total number of iterations of the experiment is n, the number of failures of the experiment has to be $(n - s)$. This is the term that is the superscript of the term $(1 - p)$, in (2.11), since $(1 - p)$ denotes the probability of failure.

Lastly, if X is a random variable, then the expected value of X is given by (2.12) and its variance is given by (2.13) below (Weisstein, "Binomial Distribution").

$$E[X] = np \tag{2.12}$$

$$Var(X) = np(1 - p) \tag{2.13}$$

As an example, assume a fair coin is tossed 100 times. The definition of a fair coin, as discussed previously, is a coin that has an equal probability of yielding a heads or a tails when tossed, with the probability being 1/2. Figures 2.3 and 2.4 below show the PMF and CDF of this binomial distribution experiment.

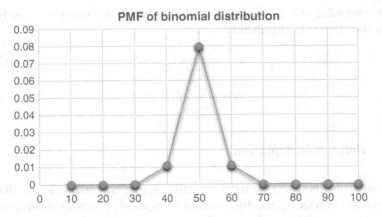

Fig. 2.3 PMF of binomial distribution of a fair coin for 100 times

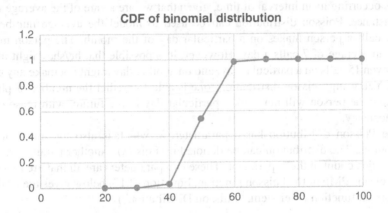

Fig. 2.4 CDF of binomial distribution of a fair coin for 100 times

2.2.3 Bernoulli Distribution

The Bernoulli distribution is a special case of the binomial distribution. In the binomial distribution, when n = 1, it is the Bernoulli distribution. The pmf of the Bernoulli distribution is given by (2.14) below (Weisstein, "Bernoulli Distribution").

$$PMF = p^{s}(1 - p)^{n-s} \qquad (2.14)$$

The parameters p, s and n are the same as that of the binomial distribution, which is probability of success, number of successful iteration yielded/desired and the total number of experimental iterations performed. If X is a random variable, then the expected value of X is given by (2.15) and its variance is given by (2.16) below (Weisstein, "Bernoulli Distribution").

$$E[X] = p \tag{2.15}$$

$$Var(X) = p(1 - p) \tag{2.16}$$

2.2.4   Poisson Distribution

The Poisson distribution is the last distribution that we will discuss in this chapter. As mentioned previously, the discussion of all types of probability distributions is beyond the scope of this book.

The Poisson distribution is one of the most versatile types of distributions that we are available. It is this distribution that can be used to model the probability of events occurring in an interval of time, given that we are aware of the average rate. For instance, Poisson distribution can be used to model the average number of phone calls a person makes on a particular day of the month. The person might make an average of 7 calls a day. However, it is possible that he/she might make 10 or even 15 calls on a particular day, and on another day might not make any calls at all. Yet, using Poisson distribution, one is able to predict the number of phone calls that the person will make on a particular day in the future, with reasonably high accuracy.

The Poisson distribution has a parameter, λ, which is also the mean of the distribution. The distribution can be denoted by Pois (λ). Another parameter, k, is the iteration count of the experiment. These two parameters are all that are required to denote the PMF of the Poisson function. Equation (2.17) below gives the PMF of the Poisson function (Weisstein, "Poisson Distribution").

$$PMF = \frac{e^{-\lambda}\lambda^k}{k!} \tag{2.17}$$

If X is a random variable, then the expected value of X is given by (2.18) and its variance is given by (2.19) below (Weisstein, "Poisson Distribution").

$$E[X] = \lambda \tag{2.18}$$

$$Var(X) = \lambda \tag{2.19}$$

Figures 2.5 and 2.6 below show the PMF and CDF of a Poisson distribution with $\lambda = 7.5$.

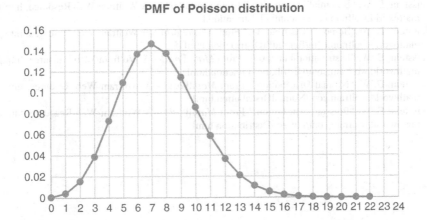

Fig. 2.5 PMF of Poisson distribution

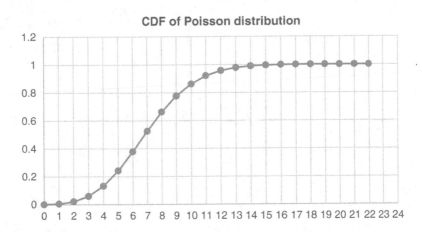

Fig. 2.6 CDF of Poisson distribution

References

Barber, D. (2012). *Bayesian reasoning and machine learning*. Cambridge, UK: University Press.

Forsyth, D., & Ponce, J. (2011). *Computer vision: A modern approach*. Upper Saddle River, NJ: Prentice Hall.

Nath, V., & Levinson, S. (2013a). *Learning to fire at targets by an iCub Humanoid Robot. AAAI Spring Symposium*. Palo Alto, CA: AAAI.

Nath, V., & Levinson, S. (2013b). *Usage of computer vision and machine learning to solve 3D mazes*. Urbana, IL: University of Illinois at Urbana-Champaign.

Nath, V., & Levinson, S. (2014). *Solving 3D mazes with machine learning: A prelude to deep learning using the iCub Humanoid Robot. 28th AAAI Conference*. Quebec City, QA: AAAI.

Weisstein, E. W. "Binomial Distribution." From *MathWorld*—A Wolfram Web Resource. http://mathworld.wolfram.com/BinomialDistribution.html

Weisstein, E. W. "Bernoulli Distribution." From *MathWorld*—A Wolfram Web Resource. http://mathworld.wolfram.com/BernoulliDistribution.html

Weisstein, E. W. "Distribution Function." From *MathWorld*—A Wolfram Web Resource. http://mathworld.wolfram.com/DistributionFunction.html

Weisstein, E. W. "Normal Distribution." From *MathWorld*—A Wolfram Web Resource. http://mathworld.wolfram.com/NormalDistribution.html

Weisstein, E. W. "Poisson Distribution." From *MathWorld*—A Wolfram Web Resource. http://mathworld.wolfram.com/PoissonDistribution.html

Chapter 3
Primer on Matrices and Determinants

Abstract In this chapter, we will be covering the basic concepts of matrices, determinants and, eigenvalues and eigenvectors in this chapter. If the reader is familiar with these concepts, then the reader can skip ahead to the next chapter without any loss of continuity.

3.1 Matrices

Matrices can be thought of as a collection of numbers, or a group of numbers, or even expressions, arranged in rows and columns. Matrices are usually rectangular in shape, although at times they can also be square in shape. Matrices are a very common way of representing a group of related numbers together, as a measurement, or to express relationships between measurements.

Each individual number or expression in a matrix is called an *element*. We just mentioned that a matrix contains rows and columns. If a matrix contains m rows and n columns, we say that the matrix has an *order of m by n*. The order of a matrix is of crucial importance in matrix operations since the size and shape of a matrix is described by the order. Furthermore, it is very important to remember that a matrix of order m by n is completely different from a matrix of order n by m. Lastly, matrices are bound by squares, but some people prefer parentheses. It doesn't matter which style the reader chooses, it is more a matter of aesthetics and not a matter of importance.

The matrix $\begin{bmatrix} 1 & 2 & 3 \\ 4 & 5 & 6 \\ 7 & 8 & 9 \end{bmatrix}$ has three rows and three columns, and therefore has an order of 3 by 3. On the other hand, the matrix $\begin{bmatrix} 1 & 2 \\ 3 & 4 \end{bmatrix}$ has two rows and two

V. Nath and S.E. Levinson, *Autonomous Military Robotics*, SpringerBriefs in Computer Science, DOI 10.1007/978-3-319-05606-7_3, © The Author(s) 2014

columns, and therefore has an order of 2 by 2. Each element in the matrix can be uniquely identified and referenced to.

The following chart shows the arrangement of elements in a 3 by 3 matrix—

$\begin{bmatrix} a_{11} & a_{12} & a_{13} \\ a_{21} & a_{22} & a_{23} \\ a_{31} & a_{32} & a_{33} \end{bmatrix}$. As can be seen, the subscript denotes the position of the element

that is being referenced, with the first number referring to the row position while the second number refers to the column position. For instance, a_{32} refers to the third row and second column, while a_{13} refers to the first row and the third column. Thus, in the aforementioned example, for the 3 by 3 matrix, $a_{11} = 1$, $a_{13} = 3$, $a_{22} = 5$, $a_{31} = 7$ and $a_{33} = 9$. In this way, every single element of any matrix can be determined and referenced without any confusion.

There are certain types of special matrices, special with regards to their size. Some matrices can have any number of rows, but only one column. They have an order of n by 1, and are called *column vectors* since they consist of only a single

column. An example of a column vector is the matrix $\begin{bmatrix} 10 \\ 20 \\ 30 \end{bmatrix}$. Some matrices can

have any number of columns, but only one row. These matrices have an order of 1 by n, and are called *row vectors* since they consist of just one row. An example of a row matrix is $\begin{bmatrix} 25 & 30 & 32 \end{bmatrix}$. Just to reiterate, the number of columns in a column vector and the number of rows in a row vector is unbounded, i.e. can be as large as required. There are certain matrices that have the same number of rows and columns. Such matrices have an order of n by n, and are also called square matrices, since they resemble the shape of a square with equal length and breadth. The matrix

that was discussed previously, $\begin{bmatrix} 1 & 2 & 3 \\ 4 & 5 & 6 \\ 7 & 8 & 9 \end{bmatrix}$, is an example of a square matrix. Of

course, even here, the number of rows and columns don't have a maximum number.

The matrix, $\begin{bmatrix} 15 & 16 & -2 & 45 \\ 0 & 99 & 56 & 7 \\ 3 & 21 & 78 & -13 \\ -1 & 17 & 81 & 22 \end{bmatrix}$, with an order of 4 by 4, also fits the definition

and is a square matrix.

In order to perform certain matrix operations, the order of the matrices involved are important, like addition and multiplication. In order to perform matrix addition between matrices, it is a requirement that both matrices must have the same order. So, in order for a matrix to be added to another matrix of order 3 by 2, the first matrix must also have an order of 3 by 2. If the order of the two matrices are the same, then it is simply a matter of addition of elements having the same position in the two matrices. The following examples should make matrix addition clear to the reader.

(i) $\begin{bmatrix} 1 & 2 & 3 \\ 4 & 5 & 6 \\ 7 & 8 & 9 \end{bmatrix} + \begin{bmatrix} 10 & 3 & 0 \\ -2 & 9 & 1 \\ 19 & 16 & 3 \end{bmatrix} = \begin{bmatrix} 11 & 5 & 3 \\ 2 & 14 & 7 \\ 26 & 24 & 12 \end{bmatrix}$

(ii) $\begin{bmatrix} 1 & 2 \\ 3 & 4 \end{bmatrix} + \begin{bmatrix} 9 & 3 \\ 4 & -1 \end{bmatrix} = \begin{bmatrix} 10 & 5 \\ 7 & 3 \end{bmatrix}$

(iii) $\begin{bmatrix} 15 & 16 & -2 & 45 \\ 0 & 99 & 56 & 7 \\ 3 & 21 & 78 & -13 \\ -1 & 17 & 81 & 22 \end{bmatrix} + \begin{bmatrix} 1 & 2 & 3 \\ 4 & 5 & 6 \\ 7 & 8 & 9 \end{bmatrix}$

= NOT POSSIBLE (ORDER MISMATCH)

Hopefully, the reader is now clear about matrix addition. The next operation is that of scalar multiplication of a matrix. The scalar multiplication of a matrix is the operation wherein a matrix is multiplied with a number. The resultant matrix is obtained when each element of the matrix is multiplied by the scalar. The following examples should hopefully throw some light on this topic for the reader.

(i) $3 * \begin{bmatrix} 1 & 2 & 3 \\ 4 & 5 & 6 \\ 7 & 8 & 9 \end{bmatrix} = \begin{bmatrix} 3*1 & 3*2 & 3*3 \\ 3*4 & 3*5 & 3*6 \\ 3*7 & 3*8 & 3*9 \end{bmatrix} = \begin{bmatrix} 3 & 6 & 9 \\ 12 & 15 & 18 \\ 21 & 24 & 27 \end{bmatrix}$

(ii) $-2 * \begin{bmatrix} 9 & 3 \\ 4 & -1 \end{bmatrix} = \begin{bmatrix} -2*9 & -2*3 \\ -2*4 & -2*-1 \end{bmatrix} = \begin{bmatrix} -18 & -6 \\ -8 & 2 \end{bmatrix}$

Another major operation that needs to be discussed is the determination of the *transpose* of a matrix. The transpose of a matrix A is denoted by $\mathbf{A}^T$. The transpose of a m by n matrix would result in a matrix with order n by m and the resultant matrix is obtained by turning all the rows of matrix A into the columns of the transpose matrix and turning all the columns of matrix A into the rows of the transpose matrix. As the keen reader would have observed by now, the transpose of a square matrix would result in a matrix with the same order as the original matrix.

(i) $\begin{bmatrix} 1 & 2 & 3 \\ 4 & 5 & 6 \\ 7 & 8 & 9 \end{bmatrix}^T = \begin{bmatrix} 1 & 4 & 7 \\ 2 & 5 & 8 \\ 3 & 6 & 9 \end{bmatrix}$

(ii) $\begin{bmatrix} 9 & 3 \\ 4 & -1 \end{bmatrix}^T = \begin{bmatrix} 9 & 4 \\ 3 & -1 \end{bmatrix}$

(iii) $\begin{bmatrix} 15 & 16 & -2 & 45 \\ 0 & 99 & 56 & 7 \\ 3 & 21 & 78 & -13 \\ -1 & 17 & 81 & 22 \end{bmatrix}^T = \begin{bmatrix} 15 & 0 & 3 & -1 \\ 16 & 99 & 21 & 17 \\ -2 & 56 & 78 & 81 \\ 45 & 7 & -13 & 22 \end{bmatrix}$

Another major matrix operation that we would discuss in this chapter is that of matrix multiplication. Matrix multiplication has a unique requirement that is different from the requirements of any of the previous requirements. The requirement is that the number of columns of the first matrix must be equal to the number of rows of the second matrix. In other words, if the order of the first matrix is m by n, then the order of the second matrix would be n by x, where x could or could not be equal to x. When these matrices are multiplied together, the resultant matrix would lead to a matrix of order m by x. In order to make things simple, the reader can imagine the two n's cancelling each other out when the two orders are being multiplied.

Once the requirements for the matrix multiplication have been satisfied, we can proceed with the actual multiplication. Basically, the first element of the resultant matrix is obtained by the piecewise multiplication of the first row of the first matrix with the left-most column of the second matrix. The second element on the first row is obtained by the multiplication of the first row of the first matrix with the second left-most column of the second matrix. This same scaling is also needed for the rows as well. In this manner, each element of the resultant matrix needs to be computed. The following examples would help the reader understand the concept of matrix multiplication better.

(i)
$$\begin{bmatrix} 1 & 2 & 3 \\ 4 & 5 & 6 \\ 7 & 8 & 9 \end{bmatrix} * \begin{bmatrix} 1 & 4 & 7 \\ 2 & 5 & 8 \\ 3 & 6 & 9 \end{bmatrix}$$

$$= \begin{bmatrix} 1*1+2*2+3*3 & 1*4+2*5+3*6 & 1*7+2*8+3*9 \\ 4*1+5*2+6*3 & 4*4+5*5+6*6 & 4*7+5*8+6*9 \\ 7*1+8*2+9*3 & 7*4+8*5+9*6 & 7*7+8*8+9*9 \end{bmatrix}$$

$$= \begin{bmatrix} 1+4+9 & 4+10+18 & 7+16+27 \\ 4+10+18 & 16+25+36 & 28+40+54 \\ 7+16+27 & 28+40+54 & 49+64+81 \end{bmatrix}$$

$$= \begin{bmatrix} 14 & 32 & 50 \\ 32 & 77 & 122 \\ 50 & 122 & 194 \end{bmatrix}$$

(ii)
$$\begin{bmatrix} 9 & 3 \\ 4 & -1 \end{bmatrix} * \begin{bmatrix} 1 & 2 \\ 3 & 4 \end{bmatrix} = \begin{bmatrix} 9*1+3*3 & 9*2+3*4 \\ 4*1+-1*3 & 4*2+-1*4 \end{bmatrix}$$

$$= \begin{bmatrix} 9+9 & 18+12 \\ 4-3 & 8-4 \end{bmatrix} = \begin{bmatrix} 18 & 30 \\ 1 & 4 \end{bmatrix}$$

(iii)
$$\begin{bmatrix} 1 & 4 & 7 \\ 2 & 5 & 8 \\ 3 & 6 & 9 \end{bmatrix} * \begin{bmatrix} 10 \\ 20 \\ 30 \end{bmatrix} = \begin{bmatrix} 1*10+4*20+7*30 \\ 2*10+5*20+8*30 \\ 3*10+6*20+9*30 \end{bmatrix}$$

$$= \begin{bmatrix} 10+80+210 \\ 20+100+240 \\ 30+120+270 \end{bmatrix} = \begin{bmatrix} 300 \\ 360 \\ 420 \end{bmatrix}$$

(iv) $\begin{bmatrix} 15 & 16 & -2 & 45 \\ 0 & 99 & 56 & 7 \\ 3 & 21 & 78 & -13 \\ -1 & 17 & 81 & 22 \end{bmatrix} * \begin{bmatrix} 1 & 4 & 7 \\ 2 & 5 & 8 \\ 3 & 6 & 9 \end{bmatrix}$

= NOT POSSIBLE (ORDER MISMATCH)

With these examples, we conclude the section on matrix multiplication. The last major matrix operation that we would discuss in this chapter is that of finding the inverse of a matrix.

For a square matrix **A**, the following (3.1) needs to be followed, to determine its inverse (Weisstein).

$$AA^{-1} = A^{-1}A = I \tag{3.1}$$

The inverse of a matrix **A** is denoted by A^{-1}. The **I** seen in (3.1) is the identity matrix, a square matrix whose elements are all 1 on the main diagonal and 0 everywhere else. For example, the 3*3 identity matrix is given below.

$$\begin{bmatrix} 1 & 0 & 0 \\ 0 & 1 & 0 \\ 0 & 0 & 1 \end{bmatrix}$$

For a 2*2 matrix $\begin{bmatrix} a & b \\ c & d \end{bmatrix}$, in order to determine its inverse, we use (3.1) and end up with (3.2) (Weisstein).

$$\begin{bmatrix} a & b \\ c & d \end{bmatrix}^{-1} = \frac{1}{ad-bc} \begin{bmatrix} d & -b \\ -c & a \end{bmatrix} \tag{3.2}$$

As an example, we will compute the inverse of the matrix $\begin{bmatrix} 1 & 2 \\ 3 & 4 \end{bmatrix}$.

$$\begin{bmatrix} 1 & 2 \\ 3 & 4 \end{bmatrix}^{-1} = \frac{1}{1*4 - 2*3} \begin{bmatrix} 4 & -2 \\ -3 & 1 \end{bmatrix} = \frac{1}{4-6} \begin{bmatrix} 4 & -2 \\ -3 & 1 \end{bmatrix}$$

$$= \frac{1}{-2} \begin{bmatrix} 4 & -2 \\ -3 & 1 \end{bmatrix} = \begin{bmatrix} -2 & 1 \\ 3/2 & -1/2 \end{bmatrix}$$

For 3*3 matrices and other matrices of greater orders, the process of computing the inverse of a matrix would still require the satisfaction of (3.1). However, it would be quite cumbersome to determine the inverse this way. Fortunately, there are other ways to determine the inverse using methods like the Gauss-Jordan method, or using minors, cofactors, etc. (Weisstein). The discussion of these topics is beyond the scope of this book and is not covered here.

3.2 Determinants

For a given *square matrix* **A**, the determinant is the volume of the transformation of the matrix A. This means that we take a hypercube of unit volume and map each vertex under the transformation, and the volume of the resultant object is defined as a determinant (Barber, 2012). Thus, the determinant of $\begin{bmatrix} 1 & 4 & 7 \\ 2 & 5 & 8 \\ 3 & 6 & 9 \end{bmatrix}$ can be computed because it is a square matrix, while the determinant of $\begin{bmatrix} 10 \\ 20 \\ 30 \end{bmatrix}$ cannot be computed because it is not a square matrix.

Let us assume a generic 3*3 matrix $\begin{bmatrix} a & b & c \\ d & e & f \\ g & h & i \end{bmatrix}$ and we shall determine its determinant. The determinant of this square matrix is written as $\begin{vmatrix} a & b & c \\ d & e & f \\ g & h & i \end{vmatrix}$, i.e. with vertical bars to denote that we are trying to determine the determinant of the matrix. The determinant of a matrix **A** is denoted by det(**A**) or also $|\mathbf{A}|$. The determinant of this matrix is given by the following equation.

$$a(e*i - f*h) - b(d*i - f*g) + c(d*h - e*g)$$

One thing to point out here is that the signs keep altering for alternating elements. The following examples would help the reader better understand the concept of determining the determinant of a matrix.

(i) $\begin{vmatrix} 1 & 4 & 7 \\ 2 & 5 & 8 \\ 3 & 6 & 9 \end{vmatrix}$

$$= 1(5*9 - 8*6) - 4(2*9 - 8*3) + 7(2*6 - 5*3)$$

$$= 1(45 - 48) - 4(18 - 24) + 7(12 - 15) = 1*(-3) + -4*(-6) + 7*(-3)$$

$$= -3 + 24 - 21 = 0$$

(ii) $\begin{bmatrix} 1 & 0 & 0 \\ 0 & 1 & 0 \\ 0 & 0 & 1 \end{bmatrix}$

$$= 1(1*1 - 0*0) - 0(0*1 - 0*0) + 0(0*0 - 1*0)$$

$$= 1 - 0 + 0$$

$$= 1$$

Of interest to note is that $\det(\mathbf{A}^T) = \det(\mathbf{A})$. Also, if two square matrices $\mathbf{A}$ and $\mathbf{B}$ are of equal dimensions, then $\det(\mathbf{AB}) = \det(\mathbf{A}) * \det(\mathbf{B})$. This section concludes a brief overview of determinants. The last section of this chapter deals with eigenvalues and eigenvectors.

3.3 Eigenvalues and Eigenvectors

The eigenvectors of a given matrix $\mathbf{A}$ correspond to a coordinate system in which the geometric transformation represented by $\mathbf{A}$ is best understood. Geometrically speaking, the eigenvectors are special directions such that the effect of the transformation $\mathbf{A}$ along a direction $\mathbf{e}$ would be to scale $\mathbf{e}$ (Barber, 2012). For a square matrix $\mathbf{a}$ of order n by n, $\mathbf{e}$ is an eigenvector of $\mathbf{a}$ with eigenvalue λ if (3.3) is satisfied.

$$ae = \lambda e \tag{3.3}$$

Equation (3.3) can be re-written as $(\mathbf{a} - \lambda*\mathbf{I})\mathbf{e} = \mathbf{0}$. This equation would have a solution if $\mathbf{e} = \mathbf{0}$, i.e. $(\mathbf{a} - \lambda*\mathbf{I})$ is invertible. In this form, the solution is trivial. There is another possibility wherein $(\mathbf{a} - \lambda*\mathbf{I})$ is non-invertible i.e. has a non-zero determinant. Therefore, λ becomes an eigenvalue of $\mathbf{a}$ if:

$$|\mathbf{a} - \lambda*\mathbf{I}| = 0 \tag{3.4}$$

Equation (3.4) is also known as the characteristic Equation. A deeper discussion of eigenvalues and eigenvectors is not required for the understanding of the material presented in this book and is being omitted here for the sake of brevity.

References

Barber, D. (2012). *Bayesian reasoning and machine learning*. Cambridge, UK: University Press.

Nath, V., & Levinson, S. (2013a). *Learning to fire at targets by an iCub Humanoid Robot. AAAI Spring Symposium*. Palo Alto, CA: AAAI.

Nath, V., & Levinson, S. (2013b). *Usage of computer vision and machine learning to solve 3D mazes*. Urbana, IL: University of Illinois at Urbana-Champaign.

Nath, V., & Levinson, S. (2014). *Solving 3D mazes with machine learning: A prelude to deep learning using the iCub Humanoid Robot. 28th AAAI Conference*. Quebec City, QC: AAAI.

Russell, S., & Norvig, P. (2010). *Artificial intelligence, a modern approach*. Upper Saddle River, NJ: Prentice Hall.

Weisstein, E. W. "Matrix Inverse." From *MathWorld*—A Wolfram Web Resource. http://mathworld.wolfram.com/MatrixInverse.html

Weisstein, E. W. "Matrix." From *MathWorld*—A Wolfram Web Resource. http://mathworld.wolfram.com/Matrix.html

3.5 Eigenvalues and Eigenvectors

$$ \tag{3.?} $$

$$ \tag{3.?} $$

References

Chapter 4
Robot Kinematics

Abstract The robotic platform is the physical hardware on which the experiments have been conducted. All algorithms, by definition, should be replicable on any physical machine, irrespective of the individual hardware components. However, all other things being constant, there is no denying that algorithms perform better on more capable hardware. In this chapter, we provide an introduction to the physical characteristics of the iCub robot platform that was used to perform the experiments and benchmark it using parameters that are relevant to the domain of robotics.

4.1 iCub Physical Description

The iCub robot is a humanoid robot that is the result of RobotCub, a collaborative project funded by the European Commission under the sixth framework programme (FP6) by Unit E5: Cognitive Systems, Interaction and Robotics. While creating an open hardware and software platform in humanoid robotics is one of the goals of the RobotCub, the primary goal of the RobotCub project is to advance the current understanding of natural and artificial cognitive systems (Metta, Sandini, Vernon, & Natale, 2008).

Standing at 1.04 m (3.41 ft) tall, the iCub is the size of a three and half year old child. The iCub is able to perform a variety of physical feats like crawling on all fours, grasp small objects like balls, etc (Nath & Levinson 2013a, 2013b). RobotCub's stance on cognition is that manipulation of objects by an agent plays a fundamental role in the development of its cognitive ability (Metta et al., 2008). However, most of such basic skills, many of which we take for granted, are not present at birth, but rather developed through ontogenesis (Metta et al., 2008). Ideally speaking, the iCub robot would push the boundaries of human understanding of cognitive development, and the primary method of doing so would be to get the iCub to interact with objects around it.

V. Nath and S.E. Levinson, *Autonomous Military Robotics*, SpringerBriefs in Computer Science, DOI 10.1007/978-3-319-05606-7_4, © The Author(s) 2014

The iCub has a total of 53 degrees of freedom (DOF), of which 30 DOF are present in the torso region. Each hand has 9 DOF with three independent fingers, and the fourth and fifth fingers have 1 DOF each since they are to be used only for providing additional stability and support. Each leg has 6 DOF and are strong enough to allow bipedal locomotion. The iCub also has a wide array of force and torque sensors, digital cameras, gyroscopes and accelerometers present inside. The low-level control loop is handled by a set of DSP-based control cards, and they all have the ability to perform full-duplex communication with each other using the CAN protocol. All the sensory and motor information is processed using an embedded Pentium-based PC104 controller. For the resource intensive operations, the computation is performed on an external cluster of machines that is connected to the iCub using a gigabit (1 gigabit $= 10^9$ bits, i.e. a billion bits) Ethernet connection (Metta et al., 2008).

4.2   DH Parameters of the iCub

A frame of reference is required to describe any physical system. One of the most commonly used convention for selecting frames of reference in robots is the Denavit-Hartenberg convention, also called the DH convention. The DH convention involves four parameters—α, θ, a and d. The names of the parameters are given below:

  (i) α—Link twist
 (ii) θ—Joint angle
(iii)   a—Link length
 (iv)   d—Link Offset

The four parameters are associated with a particular link and a particular joint. The parameter "d" is for prismatic joints, while the parameter "θ" is for revolute joints (Spong, Hutchinson, & Vidyasagar, 2006). The iCub documentation provides the DH parameters for the right hand of the iCub robot. They have been reproduced in Table 4.1 below.

Table 4.1 DH Parameters of the right arm of the iCub (Nath & Levinson 2013a, 2013b)

Link	a	d	α	θ
1	32	0	$\pi/2$	0
2	0	−5.5	$\pi/2$	−$\pi/2$
3	−23.467	−143.3	$\pi/2$	−$\pi/2$
4	0	−107.74	$\pi/2$	−$\pi/2$
5	0	0	−$\pi/2$	−$\pi/2$
6	−15	−152.28	−$\pi/2$	−$\pi/2$
7	15	0	$\pi/2$	$\pi/2$
8	0	−137.3	$\pi/2$	−$\pi/2$
9	0	0	$\pi/2$	$\pi/2$
10	62.5	16	0	π

These parameters are all components of every homogenous transformation, denoted by A. The homogenous transformation is represented as the product of four transformations, and is explained below (Spong et al., 2006).

$$A_i = Rot_{z,\theta_i} Trans_{z,d_i} Trans_{x,a_i} Rot_{x,\alpha_i}$$

$$= \begin{bmatrix} c\theta_i & -s\theta_i & 0 & 0 \\ s\theta_i & c\theta_i & 0 & 0 \\ 0 & 0 & 1 & 0 \\ 0 & 0 & 0 & 1 \end{bmatrix} \begin{bmatrix} 1 & 0 & 0 & 0 \\ 0 & 1 & 0 & 0 \\ 0 & 0 & 1 & d_i \\ 0 & 0 & 0 & 1 \end{bmatrix} \begin{bmatrix} 1 & 0 & 0 & a_i \\ 0 & 1 & 0 & 0 \\ 0 & 0 & 1 & 0 \\ 0 & 0 & 0 & 1 \end{bmatrix} \begin{bmatrix} 1 & 0 & 0 & 0 \\ 0 & c\alpha_i & -s\alpha_i & 0 \\ 0 & s\alpha_i & c\alpha_i & 0 \\ 0 & 0 & 0 & 1 \end{bmatrix}$$

$$= \begin{bmatrix} c\theta_i & -s\theta_i c\alpha_i & s\theta_i s\alpha_i & c\theta_i \\ s\theta_i & c\theta_i c\alpha_i & -c\theta_i s\alpha_i & a_i s\theta_i \\ 0 & s\alpha_i & c\alpha_i & d_i \\ 0 & 0 & 0 & 1 \end{bmatrix}$$

$$(4.1)$$

The homogenous transformation matrix that expresses the position and orientation of a set of coordinate frames with that of another set of coordinate frames is called the transformation matrix (Spong et al., 2006). If the transformation matrix expresses the set of coordinate frames j with the set i, the transformation matrix can be denoted as T_j^i, wherein

$$\begin{aligned} T_j^i &= A_{i+1} A_{i+2} \dots, \text{if } i < j \\ &= I, \qquad\qquad \text{if } i = j \\ &= \left(T_j^i\right)^{-1}, \qquad \text{if } j > i \end{aligned}$$

$$(4.2)$$

The origin of the frame of the frame of reference for the iCub robot is at the intersection point of the torso and the legs of the robot (Sandini, Metta, & Vernon, 2007). Furthermore, the iCub needs to hold out its right hand so that it can begin to shoot the target. Based on the schematics and information that were provided in the iCub documentation, we determined that the transformation matrices for 10 links would be needed, i.e. the computation of T_{10}^0 is needed. The computation was done in accordance with (4.1) and (4.2) and the results are given below.

$$T_1^0 = \begin{vmatrix} 0 & 0 & -1 & 32 \\ 0 & -1 & 0 & 5.5 \\ -1 & 0 & 0 & 0 \\ 0 & 0 & 0 & 1 \end{vmatrix}$$

$$T_2^0 = \begin{vmatrix} 0 & -1 & 0 & 175.3 \\ 1 & 0 & 0 & -17.967 \\ 0 & 0 & 1 & 0 \\ 0 & 0 & 0 & 1 \end{vmatrix}$$

$$T_3^0 = \begin{vmatrix} 1 & 0 & 0 & 175.3 \\ 0 & 0 & -1 & -17.967 \\ 0 & 1 & 0 & -107.74 \\ 0 & 0 & 0 & 1 \end{vmatrix}$$

$$T_4^0 = \begin{vmatrix} 0 & 0 & 1 & 175.3 \\ 0 & 1 & 0 & -17.967 \\ -1 & 0 & 0 & -107.74 \\ 0 & 0 & 0 & 1 \end{vmatrix}$$

$$T_5^0 = \begin{vmatrix} 0 & -1 & 0 & 175.3 \\ -1 & 0 & 0 & -17.967 \\ 0 & 0 & -1 & -107.74 \\ 0 & 0 & 0 & 1 \end{vmatrix}$$

$$T_6^0 = \begin{vmatrix} 1 & 0 & 0 & 160.3 \\ 0 & 0 & -1 & -17.967 \\ 0 & 1 & 0 & 44.54 \\ 0 & 0 & 0 & 1 \end{vmatrix}$$

$$T_7^0 = \begin{vmatrix} 0 & 0 & 1 & 160.3 \\ 0 & -1 & 0 & -17.967 \\ 1 & 0 & 0 & 59.54 \\ 0 & 0 & 0 & 1 \end{vmatrix}$$

$$T_8^0 = \begin{vmatrix} 0 & 1 & 0 & 23 \\ 1 & 0 & 0 & -17.967 \\ 0 & 0 & -1 & 59.54 \\ 0 & 0 & 0 & 1 \end{vmatrix}$$

$$T_9^0 = \begin{vmatrix} 1 & 0 & 0 & 23 \\ 0 & 0 & 1 & -17.967 \\ 0 & -1 & 0 & 59.54 \\ 0 & 0 & 0 & 1 \end{vmatrix}$$

Fig. 4.1 Position vectors of
the right arm of the iCub at
home position (Nath &
Levinson 2013a, 2013b)

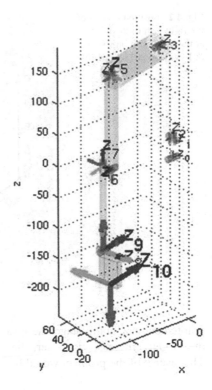

$$T_{10}^0 = \begin{vmatrix} -1 & 0 & 0 & -39.5 \\ 0 & 0 & 1 & -1.967 \\ 0 & 1 & 0 & 59.54 \\ 0 & 0 & 0 & 1 \end{vmatrix}$$

By using these transformation matrices, along with the DH parameters of the
right arm, we have all the information that is needed to get the right arm up to
slightly less than the shoulder level, getting it to the ideal level for firing the
NERF™ gun.

In order to ensure that all the calculations have been performed accurately, we
entered all the transformation matrices into a MATLAB simulator to observe the
force vectors on the right arm. In Fig. 4.1, we observe the force vectors at the instant
the right arm is at the initial phase, i.e. hanging by the torso from the shoulder at the
home position. In Fig. 4.2, we observe the force vectors of all the joints at the instant
the right arm is at the final position i.e. outstretched so that the muzzle of the gun
is in full view of the iCub. In both figures, the x axis is shown in red, the y axis is
shown in green and the z axis is shown in blue.

An analysis of all the position vectors of the joints in Fig. 4.2 provides us proof
that the calculation of the transformation matrices are accurate. It needs to be

Fig. 4.2 Position vectors of
the right arm of the iCub
at the final position (Nath
& Levinson 2013a, 2013b)

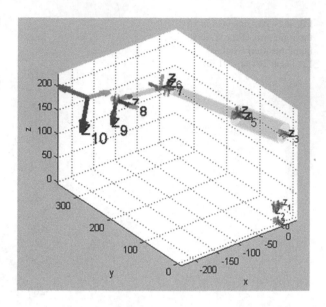

pointed out that, at this stage, the system is only in an initial stage. In order to fire at the targets progressively better, the parameters of the joints need to be altered. This aspect of the problem would be taken care of by the core algorithm itself.

References

Breazeal, C., Wang, A., & Picard, R. (2007). *Experiments with a robotic computer: Body, affect and cognition interactions. HRI'07* (pp. 153–160). Arlington, VA: ACM.

Forsyth, D., & Ponce, J. (2011). *Computer vision: A modern approach.* Upper Saddle River, NJ: Prentice Hall.

Harnad, S. (1995). *Grounding symbolic capacity in robotic capacity.* New Haven, CT: Lawrence Erlbaum.

Kormushev, P., Calinon, S., Saegusa, R., & Metta, G. (2010). Learning the skill of archery by a humanoid iCub. *2010 IEEE-RAS International Conference on Humanoid Robotics.* Nashville.

Metta, G., Sandini, G., Vernon, D., & Natale, L. (2008). The iCub humanoid robot: an open platform for research in embodied cognition. *8th Workshop on performance metrics for intelligent systems.* ACM.

Nath, V., & Levinson, S. (2013a). *Learning to fire at targets by an iCub Humanoid Robot. AAAI Spring Symposium.* Palo Alto, CA: AAAI.

Nath, V., & Levinson, S. (2013b). *Usage of computer vision and machine learning to solve 3D mazes.* Urbana, IL: University of Illinois at Urbana-Champaign.

Nath, V., & Levinson, S. (2014). *Solving 3D mazes with machine learning: A prelude to deep learning using the iCub Humanoid Robot. 28th AAAI Conference.* Quebec City, QC: AAAI.

Russell, S., & Norvig, P. (2010). *Artificial intelligence, a modern approach.* Upper Saddle River, NJ: Prentice Hall.

Sandini, G., Metta, G., & Vernon, G. (2007). The iCub cognitive humanoid robot: An open-system research platform for enactive cognition. In *50 Years of artificial intelligence* (pp. 358–369). Berlin: Springer.

Spong, M. W., Hutchinson, S., & Vidyasagar, M. (2006). *Robot modelling and control*. Hoboken, NJ: John Wiley & Sons.

Sutton, R. S., & Barto, A. G. (1998). *Reinforcement learning: An introduction*. Cambridge, UK: MIT Press.

Tsagarakis, N., Metta, G., & Vernon, D. (2007). iCUb: The design and realization of an open humanoid platform for cognitive and neuroscience research. *Advanced Robots, 21*(10), 1151–1175.

Chapter 5
Computer Vision

Abstract Image processing is required to solve the fundamental problem of determining the location of the target and the position of the gun with respect to the target. The approach that we used for the experiment, in the lab setting, was to utilize a marked static target. The target that we used for our experiment was a bulls-eye that had a yellow circular center, circumscribed by red, blue, black and white circles, radially outward in that order. All five circles were concentric in nature. The iCub robot had a stereo vision system with auto-calibration capability, making the alteration of the camera's intrinsic parameters unnecessary.

5.1 Segmentation by Thresholding

The primary approach to build the vision module was to use the segmentation by thresholding approach. At the time, it was considered to be a good idea since each target would give off a different optical intensity compared to the background objects. In this scenario, the first task was to detect the target, and then compute the centroid of the target. The centroid would be the ideal impact point of the target. In the case of the bulls-eye that was being used as the target, the centroid coincides with the center of the circles.

The image captured using the camera would be treated as an $N \times N$ array in order to create a histogram. The parameter "z" is the gray level of the particular pixel in question. $P(z)$ denotes the probability that a pixel has a gray level value z. Once the histogram has been generated, the probability is computed using (5.1) (Spong, Hutchinson, & Vidyasagar, 2006).

V. Nath and S.E. Levinson, *Autonomous Military Robotics*, SpringerBriefs in Computer Science, DOI 10.1007/978-3-319-05606-7_5, © The Author(s) 2014

$$P(z) = \frac{H[z]}{N_{rows} * N_{cols}} \qquad (5.1)$$

The camera we used supported up to a 256 color bit, so we had to compute the probabilities of z ranging from 0 to 255, using (5.1). The mean μ can be computed using (5.2).

$$\mu = \sum_{z=0}^{N-1} zP(z) \qquad (5.2)$$

Of course, (5.2) can be easily generalized using (5.1) into (5.3) given below (Spong et al., 2006).

$$\mu_i = \sum_{z=0}^{N-1} z \frac{H_i[z]}{\sum_{z=0}^{N-1} H_i[z]} \qquad (5.3)$$

Here μ_i is referred to as the conditional mean of each object.

The last mathematical parameter that needs to be computed is the variance of the gray level of the pixels. Once the mean has been computed, the variance can be computed using the equation given by

$$\sigma^2 = \sum_{z=0}^{N-1} (z - \mu)^2 P(z) \qquad (5.4)$$

As with the mean, the conditional variance for each object can also be computed.

Once these mathematical parameters have been obtained, we are ready to move on to the next phase of the algorithm, which is to divide the image into two groups—those that have a grey level below a threshold value, and those that are above the threshold value. The threshold value z_t had to be manually adjusted until a clear demarcation between the target and the background objects was obtained (Spong et al., 2006). In order to simplify the mathematical notations pertaining to the mean and variance, we decided to define $q_i(z_t)$ as the probability that a pixel in the image would belong to group i for a particular threshold value z_t. The computation of the binary values, q_0 and q_1 are computed using the set of equations given below (Spong et al., 2006).

$$q_0(z_t) = \frac{\sum_{z=0}^{z_t} H[z]}{N_{rows} * N_{cols}}$$

$$q_1(z_t) = \frac{\sum_{z=z_t+1}^{N-1} H[z]}{N_{rows} * N_{cols}}$$

With these two new parameters, we can rewrite (5.3) for both values of i, i.e. i = 0, 1 as given below (Spong et al., 2006).

$$\mu_0(z_t) = \sum_{z=0}^{z_t} z \frac{P(z)}{q_0(z_t)}$$

$$\mu_1(z_t) = \sum_{z=z_t+1}^{N-1} z \frac{P(z)}{q_1(z_t)}$$

Similarly, the equations for conditional variances are given as (5.5) and (5.6) below (Spong et al., 2006).

$$\sigma_0^2 = \sum_{z=0}^{z_t} (z - \mu_0(z_t))^2 \frac{P(z)}{q_0(z_t)} \tag{5.5}$$

$$\sigma_1^2 = \sum_{z=z_t+1}^{N} (z - \mu_1(z_t))^2 \frac{P(z)}{q_1(z_t)} \tag{5.6}$$

Now that all the required mathematical parameters have been obtained, we need to take a look at the computation of the threshold value z_t once again. At this stage, the computation is purely manual, following a hit-and-miss approach. However, such an approach is not recommended due to the potential of a wide variety of issues. We decided to follow an arithmetic approach once the variance was computed. The variance is nothing but the deviation of the value from the ideal or average value. Therefore, for a good selection of z_t, the variances would be small. The first approach would be to fit the equation (Spong et al., 2006):

$$\sigma_w^2(z_t) = q_0(z_t)\sigma_0^2(z_t) + q_1(z_t)\sigma_1^2(z_t)$$

The term σ_w^2 is known as within-group variance. While this approach works, it is computationally intensive, having to compute for N_{rows} and N_{cols}, resulting in a running time of $O(n^2)$. By making a small change in the algorithm, the running time can be brought down to $O(n)$, which is a significant boost in computing performance. The approach would be to compute the between-group variance. This variance depends on the within-group variance and the variance over the entire image, giving a much more precise answer with lower resources required. In order to compute the between-group variance, we need the values of q_0 and q_1 that were previously computed, along with their respective means. The equation to compute the between-group variance is given by

$$\sigma_b^2 = q_0(\mu_0 - \mu)^2 + q_1(\mu_1 - \mu)^2$$

This algorithm would determine the ideal value of the thresholding value z_t that would demarcate the target from the background (Spong et al., 2006). The next requirement would be to determine the centroid of the target and its orientation relative to the base reference plane. To determine these parameters, we felt that the best way would be to follow the method of moments.

Moments are basically functions defined on the image that can summarize certain aspects of the shape and size of objects in the image. The i, j moment for an object k in the image would be given by (5.7) (Spong et al., 2006).

$$m_{ij}(k) = \sum_{r,c} r^i c^j I_k(r,c) \tag{5.7}$$

In (5.7) the term (r, c) refers to the pixel values of r and c, with r being the row number and c being the column number. Also, the term I_k is called the indicator function. It gives a value of 1 when the pixel (r, c) is contained in component I, and 0 otherwise. To compute the coordinates of the centroid of component i (r', c') we use the following equation

$$r_i' = \frac{\sum_{r,c} r I_i(r,c)}{\sum_{r,c} I_i(r,c)} = \frac{m_{10}(i)}{m_{00}(i)} \tag{5.8}$$

$$c_i' = \frac{\sum_{r,c} c I_i(r,c)}{\sum_{r,c} I_i(r,c)} = \frac{m_{01}(i)}{m_{00}(i)} \tag{5.9}$$

Equations (5.8) and (5.9) can be used to compute the centroid of the given component and it can be marked by a dot or by the intersection of two lines or any other visual cue that one would like. Often, one might need moments to be computed with respect to the object center of mass. These moments are called central moments and they can be computed using (5.10).

$$C_{ij}(k) = \sum_{r,c} \left(r - r_k'\right)^i \left(c - c_k'\right)^j I_k(r,c) \tag{5.10}$$

Equation (5.10) is an important one because this equation is sufficient to give us the orientation of any component in the field of view. The orientation can be computed using (5.11) (Spong et al., 2006).

$$\tan 2\theta = \frac{2C_{11}}{C_{20} - C_{02}} \tag{5.11}$$

Figure 5.1 shows the algorithm running on several objects that have been placed together as a collection.

As can be clearly observed from Fig. 5.1, there is no way to distinguish the objects from one another. While this algorithm would be great if there no other objects other than the target in the field of view, realistically, that is not a fair requirement and other objects are almost guaranteed to be present in the frame. Therefore, an algorithm that makes more use of the known characteristics of the target was chosen to detect the target.

Fig. 5.1 Resultant centroid
on objects

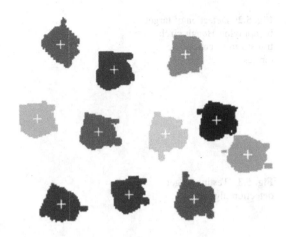

5.2 Hough Circle Transform

As mentioned before, the target was a bulls-eye that had a yellow circular center, circumscribed by red, blue, black and white circles, radially outward in that order. All five circles were concentric in nature. Due to the circular nature of the target, we decided to use the Hough circle transform to detect all objects that are circular in nature in the field of view (Lazebnik, 2013). Furthermore, the target bulls-eye contains 5 concentric circles. This means that when the Hough circle transform is run on the image, there would be 5 circles, all with the same center. This became the condition to identify a target—an object that 5 circles on it, all sharing a common point as their center.

In Fig. 5.2, we see the result of this algorithm applied to a target. The red circle indicates the boundary of the target circle, while the green dot is the computed center point. The green dot would be the perfect point of impact for the target, and is the point that has the highest reward function for the learning algorithm (details given in Sect. 6.2).

As a safety test, another test was performed on an image that contains 5 circles that are non-concentric. However, as is required, they were not classified as a target. Figure 5.3 shows the resultant image after the target detection algorithm was applied on this image.

With this, we determined that performing the Hough circle transform would be a robust method to be able to pick out targets from amongst a variety of other objects. The results of the experiment performed are examined in Chap. 8, titled "Experimental Results".

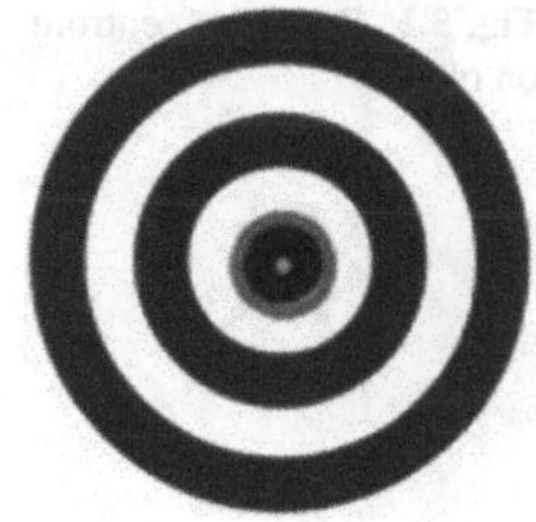

Fig. 5.2 Detection of target by applying Hough circle transform to concentric circles

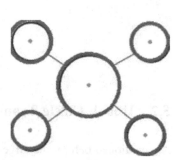

Fig. 5.3 Testing target detection algorithm

References

Begum, M., & Karray, F. (2011). Visual attention for robotic cognition: A survey. *IEEE Transactions on Autonomous Mental Development.*

Forsyth, D., & Ponce, J. (2011). *Computer vision: A modern approach.* Upper Saddle River, NJ: Prentice Hall.

Harnad, S. (1995). *Grounding symbolic capacity in robotic capacity.* New Haven, CT: Lawrence Erlbaum.

Kormushev, P., Calinon, S., Saegusa, R., & Metta, G. (2010). Learning the skill of archery by a humanoid iCub. *2010 IEEE-RAS International Conference on Humanoid Robotics.* Nashville.

Lazebnik, S. (2013). Hough Transformation [PDF Document]. Retrieved from Lecture Notes Online Web site: http://www.cs.illinois.edu/~slazebni/spring13/lec11_hough.pdf

Metta, G., Sandini, G., Vernon, D., & Natale, L. (2008). The iCub humanoid robot: an open platform for research in embodied cognition. *8th Workshop on performance metrics for intelligent systems.* ACM.

Nath, V., & Levinson, S. (2013). Learning to Fire at Targets by an iCub Humanoid Robot. *AAAI Spring Symposium.* Palo Alto, CA: AAAI.

Nath, V., & Levinson, S. (2013). *Usage of computer vision and machine learning to solve 3D mazes.* Urbana, IL: University of Illinois at Urbana-Champaign.

Nath, V., & Levinson, S. (2014). Solving 3D mazes with machine learning: A prelude to deep learning using the iCub Humanoid Robot. *28th AAAI Conference.* Quebec City, QC: AAAI.

Sandini, G., Metta, G., & Vernon, G. (2007). The iCub cognitive humanoid robot: An open-system research platform for enactive cognition. In *50 Years of artificial intelligence* (pp. 358–369). Berlin: Springer.

Spong, M. W., Hutchinson, S., & Vidyasagar, M. (2006). *Robot modelling and control.* Hoboken, NJ: John Wiley & Sons.

Tsagarakis, N., Metta, G., & Vernon, D. (2007). iCUb: The design and realization of an open humanoid platform for cognitive and neuroscience research. *Advanced Robots, 21*(10), 1151–1175.

Chapter 6
Machine Learning

Abstract Whenever a problem seems extremely open ended with a large variety of random variables that have an effect on the process, it is impossible for a human programmer to be able to account for every single case. The number of cases increases dramatically with an additional parameter. In such scenarios, probabilistic algorithms have the greatest applicability. In such scenarios, the algorithms need to be given a couple of examples of scenarios it might come across and the algorithm would be able to handle a new scenario with reasonable accuracy. The key word in the previous statement is 'reasonable'. There is no probabilistic algorithm that will always return the optimum result with a probability of 1. That would make it a deterministic algorithm which, as has just been discussed, cannot handle every potential case. In this chapter, we discuss the algorithms that were employed to successfully complete the experiment.

6.1 Overview of Machine Learning

Machine learning can be broadly thought of as the programming of an algorithm to constantly improvise itself, based on available data. However, the type of learning to be used depends a lot on the type of data being dealt with, i.e. there isn't any one size fits all policy that can be run. It is important to remember that machine learning has a probabilistic approach, i.e. it might be possible to use ML techniques to come really close to solving a problem, but it would never be able to do the task with absolute certainty. If a graph were plotted on the accuracy of machine learning based algorithms, even the best algorithms would only asymptotically approach 100 %, but never quite get there. On the other hand, if the programmer is aware of all the possible scenarios and if it is humanely possible to address all of them, then the usual programming model is recommended, wherein each individual case/state is addressed. However, we find such simple scenarios are few in number, and that scenarios that model real life would have a vast number of variables that would be too complicated to model using a computer program. It is here that the programmer needs to use machine learning techniques in order to develop an approach that would return reasonably accurate solutions.

As previously mentioned, the type of learning algorithm to be used depends on the type of the data. If the data is unlabeled, i.e. if each row of data doesn't contain any associated label with it, the data is called unlabeled data. If the data is labeled, then the data is called labeled data. For example, the weather yesterday could be represented by the vector $<1,0,1,0,1,1,1,0>$, where each digit represents a feature that is of interest. While the features have been represented, the data has not been labeled, i.e. whether this data represents a sunny or rainy or windy day. On the other hand, consider another vector $<0,1,1,1,0,0,0,$ "snow"$>$ contains a label that mentions that the data represents, which is also the desired output for any algorithm. In the former case, the data is called unlabeled data, while in the latter, the data is called labeled data.

In the case of unlabeled data, usually *clustering* takes place, i.e. elements or data points that are similar to each other tend to group together because of their common characteristics. When this takes place, the algorithm would be good at matching a new input to one of the existing clusters, although it would have no understanding whatsoever of what the data represents; the matching is based on how close the data seem to be with each clusters and then picks the closest one (Russell & Norvig, 2010). Of course, it is possible for the algorithm to go wrong, and there would no way for the algorithm to detect that it was a mistake and take corrective action. This is why the training data is very important for unlabeled data. In such a case, when there is no feedback about the accuracy of the data, the type of learning is called *unsupervised learning* (Russell & Norvig, 2010).

In the case of labeled data, the desired output is already present as part of the data itself. Therefore, it would be possible to determine a mapping function from the input to the output, based on the data provided. In this case, the algorithm would initially form a function based on the first few training examples it has seen. As it progresses through the training data, mistakes would be made and corrective action would be taken so that the mapping function can map from input to output in the best possible way. Once a function has been trained "enough", it should be able to accurately classify an unseen data point, from the test data. In reality, a function might not be able to get every single test data point accurately, and will have an error function associated with it. This method of learning is called *supervised learning* (Russell & Norvig, 2010).

There is another type of learning which seems to resemble real life much closer than the previous two types of learning that has been discussed. In the case of *reinforcement learning*, the agent learns from reinforcements that are present in the data. The goal of the agent is to achieve the stated objective, which carries the highest reward (Russell & Norvig, 2010). Paths that seem beneficial are assigned a positive reward score, while paths deemed detrimental are assigned a negative score. The agent attempts to find the path with the highest overall reward, while trying to minimize the punishment/negative reward. An interesting thing is that the optimum path might contain negative paths, or lower positive rewards than other comparable intermediate paths. Yet, the agent would attempt to try for the overall highest reward. This is very similar to our day to day lives. For instance, a lot of children might not like going to school. To them, there is no immediate benefit in attending school. On the contrary, they might consider it a punishment. However, hardly anyone of us would argue about the value of education. In the long run, a person who went to school is more likely to do well than someone who did not go to school. Therefore, although it might seem like a negative reward, children need to attend school. Similarly, plenty of people eat healthy, avoid processed and unhealthy food and exercise regularly. In the immediate short term, indulging in processed food might seem better because of the pleasant taste. People who exercise regularly might not necessarily see its benefits right away. However, in the long term, taking care of one's body is very important and achieving this might seem wasting a lot of short term happiness. We also coined a phrase "looking at the big picture" to reflect this way of thinking. All this can be mathematically modelled as reinforcement learning, and is used a lot in this book as one of the preferred machine learning algorithms. The reinforcement learning algorithms being used in this book are Q-learning and SARSA, both of which are discussed in detail in Sect. 6.3.

As aforementioned, unsupervised learning primarily includes clustering because of the lack of any labels in the data. There are other methods that also employ unsupervised learning like hidden Markov models. A detailed discussion of these topics is beyond the scope of this book and is not discussed.

Supervised learning, on the other hand, creates a mapping function from input to output that is constantly being improvised by the labeled training data. Supervised learning has a lot of applications in classification and in regression applications. One of the simplest and most commonly used classifier is the *perceptron*, which is a binary linear classifier. The perceptron converts an input, x, to an output f(x) that is either 0 or 1, based on the threshold function (Russell & Norvig, 2010). The perceptron can be trained online. A perceptron would contain a *weight vector*, **w**, which determines the weightage of the corresponding feature that it represents. Furthermore, the perceptron has a *threshold function* which is given by **Threshold (w.x)**, where

Threshold (a) = 1 if a ≥ 1, and 0 otherwise

Although the feature vector, **x**, cannot be changed, the weight vector certainly can and is dynamic in nature. As the perceptron iterates through training examples, the weight vectors converge to a solution, one that classifies the data in a linear fashion. The update equation of the weight vector is given by (6.1) below, which is also called the perceptron learning rule (Russell & Norvig, 2010).

$$w_i \leftarrow w_i + \alpha(y - threshold(x)) * x_i \qquad (6.1)$$

Another common classifier that is based on supervised learning is the *support vector machine* (SVM). It is a non-parametric method, i.e. the SVM would have to retain all the training examples. However, in practice, they might retain only a small fraction of the number of examples. SVMs construct a *maximum margin separator*, which is a decision boundary with the largest possible distance to example points. As a result, the generalization process can take place well. Furthermore, what is of great importance of SVMs is the fact that SVMs can use a *kernel function* to project points to a *higher dimensional space* in order to make them linearly separable (Russell & Norvig, 2010). This is a key difference from the perceptron which assumes that all the data points are linearly separable.

There are several other types of classifiers that are based on supervised learning. One of the other common ones are the neural networks. The neural networks are composed of nodes that are connected by links. A link from one node to the next is to propagate the activation from node 1 to node 2, and a weight w that is associated with the weightage given to that link. Each node's input is taken as the weighted sum of all its inputs. The output of the node is based on an *activation function* which could be a hard threshold or a logistic function. If it is a hard threshold, the node is called *perceptron* (discussed above) and if it is a logistic function, then the node is called *sigmoid perceptron* (Russell & Norvig, 2010). Other types of classifiers include Naïve Bayes', decision trees, linear regression and logistic regression. A detailed discussion of these classifiers, as well as other machine learning concepts, is beyond the scope of this book. Interested readers are encouraged to read the books mentioned in the References section for detailed information about machine learning concepts.

6.2   Least Mean Square Approximation

If the target is stationery, the vision system would be able to detect the point of impact of the bullet on the target area. Also, the vision system would be able to determine the center of the target area using the Hough circle transform (explained in Sect. 5.1). In the event that the bullet missed the mark, there are two errors that need to be determined in order to make the next shot more accurate. The two errors are the radial and translational errors. The two errors are determined by (6.2) and (6.3) respectively.

$$\varepsilon_\theta = \left\| \theta' - \theta \right\| \tag{6.2}$$

$$\varepsilon_r = \left\| r' - r \right\| \tag{6.3}$$

After the determination of the radial and translational errors using (6.2) and (6.3) after the first iteration, the next goal is to alter the joint angles so that both the errors converge to 0. An error of 0 implies that the point of impact of the bullet exactly superimposes the center of the target i.e. a perfect shot. In practice, it is extremely difficult to get a situation where both errors are of magnitude 0. The requirement is that with each iteration, the errors keep converging to 0, so that we are assured of a progressively improving model. The results obtained by utilizing this LMS method is discussed in Chap. 8.

6.3 Reinforcement Learning

For dynamic targets, the LMS approach described in Sect. 6.2 will not work. This is because the errors are designed to be measured against a common frame of reference. However, with a moving target, the frame of reference is not present. The problem is compounded even further when the target does not move in a fixed pattern i.e. it does not want to be hit and tries its best to evade the bullet. In such a case, a learning algorithm needs to be implemented so that the iCub can utilize its past experiences as a point of reference and predict the location of the target after a set time interval. By being able to predict the position of the target, the probability of actually hitting the target with a bullet increases.

The most robust learning algorithm that is resilient to noise is the Q-learning algorithm (Russell & Norvig, 2010). In order to apply the Q-learning algorithm, we set an extremely high reward for accurately hitting the target, an increasing penalty as the distance from the point of impact to the center increases radially (based on the errors mentioned in Sect. 6.2) and also a penalty for the time it takes to fire a shot. In this way, the iCub attempts to obtain a control policy that would result in firing the most accurate shot in the least amount of time.

The update equation for temporal difference Q-learning is given by (6.4) below (Russell & Norvig, 2010).

$$Q(s,a) \leftarrow Q(s,a) + \alpha\Big(R(s) + \gamma \max_{a'} Q\big(s',a'\big) - Q(s,a)\Big) \qquad (6.4)$$

Where α is the learning rate and γ is the discount factor.

Upon closer examination of (6.4), we observe that Q-learning backs up the best Q-value from the state that was reached in the observed transition. In other words, Q-learning does not pay any attention to the actual policy being followed. Therefore, it is also called an off-policy algorithm and so it would not generate a policy that would maximize the probability of hitting the target. However, there is clearly a need to maximize this probability and an on-policy algorithm is required. The SARSA algorithm seemed like a good choice since it was very similar to the Q-learning algorithm, but was an on-policy algorithm. The update equation for SARSA is given by (6.5) below (Russell & Norvig, 2010).

$$Q(s,a) \leftarrow Q(s,a) + \alpha\Big(R(s) + \gamma\, Q\big(s',a'\big) - Q(s,a)\Big) \qquad (6.5)$$

While the difference between (6.4) and (6.5) may seem very subtle at first, there is a pretty significant difference between Q-learning and the SARSA algorithm. The SARSA algorithm actually waits until an action is taken and then updates the Q-value for that action. Simply put, if a greedy agent that always takes the action with the best Q-value is required, Q-learning is the algorithm to use. However, if exploration of the state space is required, SARSA is the algorithm that offers a lot more advantages. For the purposes of this experiment, an exploratory algorithm is required to maximize the probability to hit the target accurately. Therefore, we decided to go with the SARSA algorithm. The optimum policy for the SARSA is given by (6.6) below.

$$\pi^* = argmax_\pi \sum\nolimits_h P(h|\ e) u_h^\pi. \qquad (6.6)$$

In (6.6), the posterior probability P(h|e) is obtained by using the Bayes' rule and applying it to the observations that have been obtained. This is how the feedback loop that allows constant improvisation with each iteration is created.

References

Barber, D. (2012). *Bayesian reasoning and machine learning*. Cambridge, UK: Cambridge University Press.

Breazeal, C., Wang, A., & Picard, R. (2007). *Experiments with a robotic computer: Body, affect and cognition interactions*. *HRI'07* (pp. 153–160). Arlington, VA: ACM.

Buşoniu, L., Babuška, R., De Schutter, B., & Ernst, D. (2010). *Reinforcement learning and dynamic programming using function approximators*. New York: CRC Press.

Harnad, S. (1995). *Grounding symbolic capacity in robotic capacity*. New Haven, CT: Lawrence Erlbaum.

Kormushev, P., Calinon, S., Saegusa, R., & Metta, G. (2010). Learning the skill of archery by a humanoid iCub. *2010 IEEE-RAS International Conference on Humanoid Robotics*. Nashville.

Metta, G., Sandini, G., Vernon, D., & Natale, L. (2008). The iCub humanoid robot: an open platform for research in embodied cognition. *8th Workshop on performance metrics for intelligent systems*. ACM.

Michalski, C., & Mitchell, T. (1983). *Machine learning*. Palo Alto, CA: Tioga Publishing Company.

Michie, D. (1986). *On machine intelligence*. New York: John Wiley & Sons.

Nath, V., & Levinson, S. (2013). Learning to Fire at Targets by an iCub Humanoid Robot. *AAAI Spring Symposium*. Palo Alto, CA: AAAI.

Nath, V., & Levinson, S. (2013). *Usage of computer vision and machine learning to solve 3D mazes*. Urbana, IL: University of Illinois at Urbana-Champaign.

Nath, V., & Levinson, S. (2014). Solving 3D mazes with machine learning: A prelude to deep learning using the iCub Humanoid Robot. *28th AAAI Conference*. Quebec City, QC: AAAI.

Russell, S., & Norvig, P. (2010). *Artificial intelligence, a modern approach*. Upper Saddle River, NJ: Prentice Hall.

Sandini, G., Metta, G., & Vernon, G. (2007). The iCub cognitive humanoid robot: An open-system research platform for enactive cognition. In *50 Years of artificial intelligence* (pp. 358–369). Berlin: Springer.

Sigaud, O., & Buffet, O. (2010). *Markov decision processes in artificial intelligence*. New York: Wiley.

Sutton, R. S., & Barto, A. G. (1998). *Reinforcement learning: An introduction*. Cambridge, UK: MIT Press.

Tsagarakis, N., Metta, G., & Vernon, D. (2007). iCUb: The design and realization of an open humanoid platform for cognitive and neuroscience research. *Advanced Robots, 21*(10), 1151–1175.

Chapter 7
Bullet Kinematics

Abstract A key component that needs an in-depth analysis is the kinematics of the bullet that is being fired. While most bullets would work over a very short range, the difficulty begins to increase exponentially as the distance to the target increases. Even weather-related factors like wind speed and humidity can affect the accuracy of the shot. It is said that a sniper even needs to consider factors like the Coriolis Effect and the curvature of the earth to get an accurate shot. In the experimental setup we created, we did not attempt to snipe people at long range! On the contrary, we used commercially available a NERF™ gun and NERF™ bullets to simulate the firing of the gun and the motion of the bullet. The analysis that is presented in this chapter is for the NERF™ gun and bullet only.

7.1 Determination of Bullet Speed

The determination of every single parameter to model a bullet's trajectory is beyond the scope of the experimental resources we had at the time. As a result, we used the equations of motion and simple math to derive all the parameters that we required. In order to avoid the effects of air pressure, temperature changes and wind conditions, all the experiments to determine the bullet kinematics were performed indoors under laboratory conditions.

The first step is to determine the horizontal velocity of the bullet. In order to do so, one needs to fire a bullet and determine the distance the bullet traversed and the time taken to perform that traversal. Table 7.1 below shows the results that were obtained during the experiment.

As can be seen from the experimental results that have been tabulated above, the horizontal velocity of the bullet can be estimated to be around 2.77 m/s with a standard deviation of 0.85 m/s. However, the sample size is not large enough to account for all possible scenarios. Furthermore, it needs to be reiterated that the

Table 7.1 Experimental results of the distance travelled by NERF™ bullet and the time taken

Serial Number9.	Distance (m)	Time (s)	Speed (m/s)
1	5.86	2.07	2.83
2	5.78	2.11	2.74
3	5.79	2.09	2.77
4	5.92	2.03	2.92
5	5.82	2.09	2.78
6	5.77	2.12	2.72
7	5.85	2.1	2.79
8	5.91	2.05	2.88
9	5.84	2.09	2.79
10	5.82	2.07	2.81
11	5.71	2.04	2.80
12	5.92	2.22	2.67
13	5.85	2.1	2.79
14	5.88	1.98	2.97
15	5.85	2.4	2.44
16	5.83	2.08	2.80
17	5.62	2.02	2.78
18	5.78	2.13	2.71
19	5.94	2.18	2.72
20	5.81	2.04	2.85
Average	5.83	2.10	2.77
Std. Dev.	0.08	0.09	0.85

experiment was performed indoors and therefore does not account for wind conditions, air pressure, temperature changes and any other environmental factors.

The trajectory of a bullet follows a parabolic path. The bullet has an initial velocity of 0 m/s and then travels a horizontal distance, while falling through a vertical distance under the influence of gravity. The bullet was launched from the NERF™ gun while the iCub was holding it at a shoulder level position. The height of the muzzle was 0.93 m from the floor. Using the equations of motion, we can determine the expected vertical displacement of the bullet, ignoring air resistance. Based on all this information, we decided to place the stationery target at a distance of 2 m away from the iCub. At such a distance, the vertical displacement is within a tolerable limit i.e. the bullet has a high probability of making contact with the target surface so that the iCub can measure the error. It would be a different scenario if the bullet falls on the ground and the iCub keeps waiting for a bullet to make contact with the target surface, leading to a potential infinite waiting period. Of course, this can be avoided by setting a time limit, but we feel that this does not match the scope of the research experiment. Furthermore, at this distance the NERF™ bullet still has enough energy to strike the target with sufficient force, so that it would remain stuck to the target (Nath & Levinson, 2013a). This is important because the vision algorithm needs to determine the point of impact of the bullet and this information is needed to compute the error and further adjust the parameters for a more successful shot (see Sect. 6.2).

References

Kormushev, P., Calinon, S., Saegusa, R., & Metta, G. (2010). Learning the skill of archery by a humanoid iCub. *2010 IEEE-RAS International Conference on Humanoid Robotics*. Nashville.

Metta, G., Sandini, G., Vernon, D., & Natale, L. (2008). The iCub humanoid robot: an open platform for research in embodied cognition. *8th Workshop on performance metrics for intelligent systems*. ACM.

Nath, V., & Levinson, S. (2013a). Learning to Fire at Targets by an iCub Humanoid Robot. *AAAI Spring Symposium*. Palo Alto, CA: AAAI.

Nath, V., & Levinson, S. (2013b). *Usage of computer vision and machine learning to solve 3D mazes*. Urbana, IL: University of Illinois at Urbana-Champaign.

Nath, V., & Levinson, S. (2014). Solving 3D mazes with machine learning: A prelude to deep learning using the iCub Humanoid Robot. *28th AAAI Conference*. Quebec City, QC: AAAI.

Sandini, G., Metta, G., & Vernon, G. (2007). The iCub cognitive humanoid robot: An open-system research platform for enactive cognition. In *50 Years of artificial intelligence* (pp. 358–369). Berlin: Springer.

Spong, M. W., Hutchinson, S., & Vidyasagar, M. (2006). *Robot modelling and control*. Hoboken, NJ: John Wiley & Sons.

Tsagarakis, N., Metta, G., & Vernon, D. (2007). iCUb: The design and realization of an open humanoid platform for cognitive and neuroscience research. *Advanced Robots, 21*(10), 1151–1175.

Chapter 8
Experimental Results

Abstract In this chapter, we discuss the experimental results of the application of all the modules that have been described in this book to firing toy bullets at a bulls-eye target. The iCub utilizes the Hough circle transform, mentioned in Sect. 3.2 to identify targets. Also, the targets are static, employing the LMS approach.

8.1 Experimental Results and Its Analysis

Figure 8.1 shows the NERF™ bullet's point of impact (top right side) on the target. The setup was then allowed to run for as long as needed, without any external interference. We were surprised to see an extremely accurate shot on the target by the 6th iteration. In Fig. 8.2, the impact of the final NERF™ bullet right on the center of the target shows that even a simple approach like the least mean squares approach is a very accurate approach to hit stationery targets. In Fig. 8.2, the reader might be able to see only 3 bullets and not 6. This is because 3 bullets fell off after a few seconds because the sticky tape at their end wasn't strong enough. However, this did not affect the experiment since we made sure that the robot was able to determine their point of impact and make necessary corrections before the bullets fell off.

The following sequences of images of the iCub were taken during the execution of the experiment. It is our hope that the reader might find it interesting!

V. Nath and S.E. Levinson, *Autonomous Military Robotics*, SpringerBriefs in Computer Science, DOI 10.1007/978-3-319-05606-7_8, © The Author(s) 2014

Fig. 8.1 First iteration

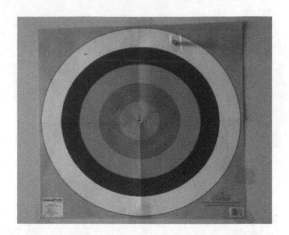

Fig. 8.2 After a few
iterations

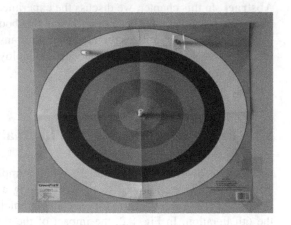

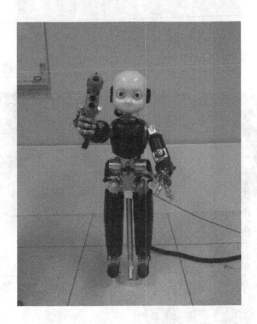

Chapter 9
Future Direction

While having humanoid robots that fire guns as effectively as the clones in Star Wars: The Attack of the Clones might be a distant reality, we believe that, as of now, the technology has developed enough to begin developing simplistic prototypes. The development of such robots would be a quantum leap forward in protecting our nation's national security as well as for law enforcement.

The work described in this book has described every module that needs to be implemented in order to have a humanoid robot fire at a static target using a commercially available toy gun. The book also explains how Q-learning may be employed in order to deal with randomly-moving targets. The work that has been presented in this book is intended only as a starting point for work in this direction. More sophisticated algorithms will need to be employed in order to deal with a wide variety of unknown variables.

In terms of future direction, a lot more research needs to be undertaken in order to develop extremely accurate algorithms for target detection. The importance of this point cannot be stressed enough, since picking out a wrong target by a fully armed autonomous robot would result in the death or severe injury of (a) person (s) and damage to property. While picking out targets in an isolated environment is fairly trivial, the challenge would be to pick out targets in a crowded environment, where other entities with features similar to what the target possesses are in close proximity to the target.

Another area that deserves a lot of research focus is in the combination of the environmental factors and optimizing the bullet trajectory's probability of making impact with the target. In the work presented, all the experiments took place in a laboratory setting where the effect of external environmental factors were minimized to the maximum possible extent. However, in a real combat situation, the scenario is extremely different from that of a lab environment. There are a lot more factors to consider like wind speed and direction, poor visibility due to weather conditions like rain or fog, humidity and a variety of other environmental factors.

Of special mention is the possible misuse of such autonomous robots by people in authority and even malicious hackers. The robots could possibly be used for subjugation of people and for other illegal and unethical activities. Utmost care

V. Nath and S.E. Levinson, *Autonomous Military Robotics*, SpringerBriefs in Computer Science, DOI 10.1007/978-3-319-05606-7_9, © The Author(s) 2014

must be undertaken in order to make sure that the robots would never be used on innocent civilians and safety mechanisms that prevent any such incident from occurring is a core requirement. However, even for legitimate purposes, there needs to be flexibility in order to determine potential targets by a human user. This requirement makes the strict enforcement of safety mechanisms a design issue and needs to be taken into account by the law makers and the officials in charge of the robots themselves. While a case involving the potential misuse of such robots is a scary scenario, if used only for legitimate purposes, the development of such robots would be a great step forward towards building a better society and planet.

References

Asimov, I. (1991). *I, Robot*. New York, NY: Spectra, Mti Edition.

Harnad, S. (1995). *Grounding symbolic capacity in robotic capacity*. New Haven, CT: Lawrence Erlbaum.

Kormushev, P., Calinon, S., Saegusa, R., & Metta, G. (2010). Learning the skill of archery by a humanoid iCub. *2010 IEEE-RAS International Conference on Humanoid Robotics*. Nashville.

Metta, G., Sandini, G., Vernon, D., & Natale, L. (2008). The iCub humanoid robot: an open platform for research in embodied cognition. *8th Workshop on performance metrics for intelligent systems*. ACM.

Michalski, C., & Mitchell, T. (1983). *Machine learning*. Palo Alto, CA: Tioga Publishing Company.

Michie, D. (1986). *On machine intelligence*. New York, NY: Wiley.

Nath, V., & Levinson, S. (2013). Learning to Fire at Targets by an iCub Humanoid Robot. *AAAI Spring Symposium*. Palo Alto: AAAI.

Nath, V., & Levinson, S. (2013). *Usage of computer vision and machine learning to solve 3D mazes*. Urbana, IL: University of Illinois at Urbana-Champaign.

Nath, V., & Levinson, S. (2014). Solving 3D mazes with machine learning: A prelude to deep learning using the iCub Humanoid Robot. *28th AAAI Conference*. Quebec City, QC: AAAI.

Russell, S., & Norvig, P. (2010). *Artificial intelligence, a modern approach*. Upper Saddle River, NJ: Prentice Hall.

Sandini, G., Metta, G., & Vernon, G. (2007). The iCub cognitive humanoid robot: An open-system research platform for enactive cognition. In *50 Years of artificial intelligence* (pp. 358–369). Berlin: Springer.

Spong, M. W., Hutchinson, S., & Vidyasagar, M. (2006). *Robot modelling and control*. Hoboken, NJ: John Wiley & Sons.

Tsagarakis, N., Metta, G., & Vernon, D. (2007). iCUb: The design and realization of an open humanoid platform for cognitive and neuroscience research. *Advanced Robots, 21*(10), 1151–1175.

Wells, H. (2005). *The war of the worlds*. New York, NY: NYRB Classics.